essentials

Managing
Your Money

Time-saving books that teach specific skills to busy people, focusing on what really matters; the things that make a difference – the *essentials*.

Other books in the series include:

Business Letters that Work

Expand Your Vocabulary

Preparing a Marketing Plan

Leading Teams

Making the Most of Your Time

Solving Problems

Coaching People

Hiring People

Making Great Presentations

Writing Good Reports

The Ultimate Business Plan

Writing Business E-mails

Managing
Your Money

John Claxton

ESSENTIALS

To Finn and Sophie

Published in 2001 by
How To Books Ltd, 3 Newtec Place,
Magdalen Road, Oxford OX4 1RE, United Kingdom
Tel: (01865) 793806   Fax: (01865) 248780
e-mail: info@howtobooks.co.uk
www.howtobooks.co.uk

British Library Cataloguing in Publication Data.
A catalogue record for this book is available from
the British Library.

Edited by Francesca Mitchell
Cover design by Shireen Nathoo Design
Produced for How To Books by Deer Park Productions
Typeset by PDQ Typesetting, Newcastle-under-Lyme, Staffordshire
Printed and bound in Great Britain by Bell & Bain Ltd., Glasgow

NOTE: The material contained in this book is set out in good faith for
general guidance and no liability can be accepted for loss or expense
incurred as a result of relying in particular circumstances on
statements made in the book. Laws and regulations are complex
and liable to change, and readers should check the current position
with the relevant authorities before making personal arrangements.

ESSENTIALS *is an imprint of*
How To Books

Contents

Introduction

Personal finance is a very wide subject. The object of this book is to draw attention to the most important matters you should consider in order to manage your money well.

It is a book for dipping into rather than reading from cover to cover, but I recommend all readers to carry out the ten-point financial health check, as explained in the first chapter. Then you can compare your position with the ideal. The rest of the book will help you improve any areas where you fall short.

It makes no different whether you are wealthy or struggling to make ends meet; you should find something here to help you improve your financial position.

The money world is always changing and the information in the book can only be up to date at the time of publication; it is best to check before taking action.

Some figures are liable to change each year in the budget. This edition includes those introduced in the March 2001 budget.

John Claxton

1 Formulating Your Money Strategy

Before you can start to manage your money you need to check where you stand.

In this chapter, four things that really matter:
- ~ Preparing background information
- ~ Doing your financial health check
- ~ Making strategic decisions
- ~ Analysing your savings needs

Unless you are qualified, you cannot be your own doctor, but with some help you can be your own financial adviser.

Carrying out a financial health check is the first stage in managing your money and is the cornerstone of this book. It is rather like the 'fact-find' that a financial adviser carries out on a new client, but is much wider in scope.

A financial adviser will ask you for certain background information. You already know all this but you need to bear it in mind as you do the check.

Having made the check, you can plan the action you need to take in order to get yourself up to par. This may well include the need to save.

Is this you?

• My finances are in a mess and I don't know what to sort out first. • I think insurance is a waste of money. • I'm too young to worry about a pension. • I wish I could afford a holiday. • I can save a bit each month but I just put it in the building society. • How can I make sure my children get all my savings when I die and not the Chancellor?

Preparing background information

Personal profile

A financial adviser will ask you your age, whether you are employed, self-employed, unemployed or retired, whether you are married, have children still dependent on you (or any other dependents, such as a widowed mother without much pension) and what is your highest income tax rate (your marginal rate).

Budgeting

If you do not have a clear idea of your weekly or monthly income and expenditure, prepare a budget. Include in it any savings you are making for a specific event.

Your financial assets and liabilities

List any savings and investments you have, followed by a list of any liabilities, such as bank overdraft or credit card debt. The difference between the two is the value of your net current assets (if it is a negative amount, you need to plan to reduce your debt).*

Doing your financial health check

* You now know more clearly whether you are able to save in order to improve your financial health.

The ten steps which follow are in order of priority.

~ Reducing borrowing

Are you borrowing money, except against your home? If so, consider paying it off as soon as possible.

~ Establishing a cash reserve

Have you got a cash reserve to fall back on – at least one month's normal expenditure and preferably two or three, in a deposit account?*

~ Avoiding financial disaster

Is your income protected by insurance against the death, sickness or permanent disability of the breadwinner? Do you have adequate home and car insurance?

~ Retirement planning

Are you paying towards a pension? It is never too early nor too late to start.

~ Getting tax and social security advantages

Are you getting all the income tax allowances, reliefs and credits, and social security benefits you are entitled to?

If you do not have a cash reserve and all your spare cash is being used to reduce debt, do you have a borrowing facility?

~ Paying for education

If you have young children, are you saving up to pay for private education and/or university?

~ Saving for special events

Do you need to save up for your next holiday, a new car or a wedding? Putting aside just a small amount regularly is the best way.

~ Reducing your mortgage

It is worth considering a reduction before investing surplus income.

~ Investment planning

Do you have surplus income which can be channelled into a savings scheme or do you have a lump sum to invest?

~ Estate planning

Will your heirs have to pay inheritance tax? If so, consider how to avoid it or pay for it yourself.

Making strategic decisions

The result of your financial health check may cause you to change your budget, for example to pay for more insurance cover.

Or you may wish to change your existing savings and investments to fit in with these guidelines – perhaps to put more into your cash reserve.*

Analysing your savings needs

If you need or wish to save, consider the following:

~ What are you saving for – to increase your cash reserve, for a special event, for your children's education, for retirement – and how much do you need?

~ How much can you save each week or month and how long will it therefore take to achieve your objective?

~ Do you need quick access to the money, bearing in mind that you might get a higher return if not?

* *After all that, you may still have a need and an ability to save.*

~ Do you pay tax and, if so, what is your marginal rate? Compare returns on an after-tax basis.

~ Can you save regularly? Irregular deposits when you can afford them are better than nothing.*

~ Is your priority income or capital growth? Some investments are better for one, some for the other, but many achieve both.

~ How much risk are you prepared to take? Higher risk should lead to higher returns, but only in the longer term.

Summary points

★ A financial health check is the first and most important step towards managing your money.

* Be wary of committing yourself to a regular savings contract if there is a penalty for missing a payment.

★ Start from where you are now by preparing budgets and listing any existing savings and investments.

★ How does your present position compare with the ideal and how can you bridge the gap.

★ If you are saving, you need to decide what you are saving for, so that you invest appropriately.

2 Managing Your Cash

Cash is the sharp end of your monetary affairs.

In this chapter, six things that really matter:
- ~ Accumulating an emergency fund
- ~ Managing borrowing
- ~ Controlling debt
- ~ Reducing your mortgage
- ~ Running your bank accounts
- ~ Managing your credit cards

Cash comes and goes so quickly that it is vital to get it under control and also to make sure that it is always working for you, earning interest whilst in your hands.

Compare interest rates available by finding out the AER – annual equivalent rate. (In the case of borrowed money, it is called the APR – annual percentage rate – but is effectively the same.) These comparable rates allow for the timing of receipts/payments, whether of interest or capital.

In this way you are recognising the time value of money, which simply means that cash in hand today has more value to you than if you have to wait for it.

Is this you?

• Whenever I need extra money I have to take up a bank overdraft. • I always owe money on my credit card but the interest doesn't seem much. • How can I get more interest on my savings? • Should I use my bonus to reduce my mortgage? • My bank is never open when I need it.

Accumulating an emergency fund

Building it up

You should have at least one month's income in your cash reserve, preferably more. The alternative, only applicable if you are paying off debt or building up your reserve is a borrowing facility – that is, a source of emergency finance from somewhere else. This could be a bank overdraft facility or unused credit card balance.

The trouble with these facilities is that if you use them they are expensive, so you need to build up your emergency fund as soon as possible.

Another potential facility is your immediate family; would your parents, for example, be able and willing to make a temporary loan?

Depositing it safely

Use a bank or building society deposit account. Instant access is best, even though higher rates of interest are available on notice accounts, because the money might be needed in a hurry.

Higher rates are usually available on higher amounts, so it is worth using the same account for any short-term savings such as for your holiday. Postal and Internet accounts often offer higher rates.

Rates change and it is important to check regularly. Comparisons of rates can be found in newspapers, money magazines and on the Internet.*

Remember to compare rates of interest by using the AER (annual equivalent rate) to take account of the timing of interest payments.

Managing borrowing

Recognising types of credit

There are many ways of borrowing money. The two important things are the rate of interest (the APR) and whether you have any extra time to pay if you fall behind.

Bank current account overdraft

An authorised overdraft has the advantage that interest is calculated on a daily basis, so as your pay reaches your account the amount of overdraft, and so the interest on it, reduces. The disadvantage is that the bank can withdraw the facility at any time.

There may be a fee to pay, as well as interest. The usual interest rate is around 5% above bank base rate (the rate fixed by the Bank of England and reviewed each month, at the time of going to press, 5.25%). Avoid unauthorised overdrafts – they can be very expensive.

Bank personal loan

Above a certain amount, a bank will not grant

an overdraft but instead may provide a personal loan, which has the advantage that it cannot be withdrawn once started. The interest rate is about the same but is payable on the full amount outstanding.

Credit card

If you time your payments well, you can get nearly two months' free credit. Otherwise, subject to the payment of 10% of the outstanding balance each month, you can have continuing credit – at a cost. The APR on credit cards may be 10% above bank base rate.

Shop credit

Some shops may from time to time offer credit on a purchase. Make sure it is good value for money.*

Loan from employer

Some employers make loans available to employees, such as for season tickets, and they may be interest-free. A loan above £5,000 is taxable, but paying the tax on an

* Always check the APR.

interest-free loan is cheaper than paying the interest!

Borrowing against a life assurance policy

If you have a life policy and need a loan, this route is well worth considering, as the rate of interest should be lower than a bank loan or overdraft.

Second mortgage

This will be cheaper than other forms of borrowing (about 2% above base rate) because of the security. But there will be charges to pay, so it is only suitable for the longer term.

Re-mortgage

This is an increase in your house mortgage. It is the cheapest form of loan but again there will be charges, so it is a long-term proposition.

Credit checklist

If you intend borrowing money, run through these questions:

~ What is the interest rate, expressed as APR, and is it fixed or variable?

~ How much can you afford to repay, weekly or monthly, and so how long will it take to pay it off the loan?

~ Flexibility: can you pay it off early and what happens if you are temporarily unable to pay?

~ Is there any other risk? For example, is your home put up as security against the loan?

~ Are any fees payable ?

If you are not required to make regular repayments but have to wait till the end of the loan period, open a savings account to build up the repayment.*

* *If you are really desperate, credit brokers can help you find a loan, but beware of loan sharks. Make sure you know the APR before signing up.*

Controlling debt

If you get into trouble with repayments, the best thing is to contact your lender immediately – they may offer a solution. If not, try your local Citizens' Advice Bureau or telephone National Debtline – 0121 359 8501; both give free advice.

Licensed debt practitioners will help you to get out of trouble with debt, but be careful because there is no control over them. Any new credit they arrange might give rise to worse problems. Check the APR.

If you are paying extortionate interest you can get redress through the courts.*

Reducing your mortgage

A mortgage used to help buy your home is a long-term loan. It is secured on your property and involves the payment of interest and some arrangement to repay the loan, either by instalments (a repayment mortgage) or by a lump-sum payment at the end, from an endowment policy, the lump sum from your pension, or PEP/ISA investments.

Although the interest rate is usually only some 2% above bank base rate, there is some advantage in paying it off early. It is unlikely that you will be able to get a higher return by investing the money.

* *If you have a bad credit reference and it is not justified, there are ways of getting it changed – contact the Citizens' Advice Bureau.*

You need to have a mortgage that is flexible enough to let you make additional repayments without penalty.

If you have a repayment mortgage, check whether the interest is calculated daily or once a year. If it's once a year, time your repayment just before the relevant date.

Running your bank accounts

Most people have a current account to handle their cash transactions. Many couples have a joint account, usually on a one-signature basis.

Bank cards

These guarantee payments of a cheque for up to £50 or £100. They can also be used for cash withdrawals from cash machines. Watch out for charges for using the machines of some other banks.

Your card may be extended to the Cirrus system, whereby you can withdraw cash abroad wherever you see the Cirrus symbol, the charge being 2% in addition to the exchange rate difference.

Debit cards

Your bank card usually doubles as a debit card – either Delta or Switch. When it is used, your account is debited immediately. There must be sufficient funds in your account, but there are no charges.

Debit cards are an easy way to pay and do impose a form of self-control not available with a credit card. Also you can use the card to get 'cash back', usually limited to £50, at supermarkets.

The card may be extended to the Maestro system, enabling you to use it abroad wherever you see the symbol, the cost being 2% plus the exchange rate difference (probably more than the cost of using a credit card).

Standing orders and direct debits

Standing orders are instructions to your bank to pay a set amount on a set date. Direct debits are instructions to your bank to pay to a specified commercial organisation any amount requested by them at any time.

The disadvantage of a direct debit is that you lose control: if the other party makes a mistake it can be difficult to get it rectified.

Charges and interest

Currently many banks pay a small interest rate on current accounts and do not impose charges for the services so far discussed, but this could change.

There are charges for other services, such as a 'bounced' cheque, where there are insufficient funds in your account to meet it, or an overdraft (especially if unauthorised).*

Telephone and Internet banking

These have the advantage of being available at any time on any day. Internet banking has the added advantage of displaying recent transactions.

Managing your credit cards

A credit card is an easy way to pay without carrying large amounts of cash. It saves

* Make sure you know the time it takes for your bank to clear a cheque, i.e. to find out that it has been accepted by the payee's bank – usually three or four days.

writing cheques and, best of all, it can give between one and two months' free credit. Also, if the card is used to buy goods or services in excess of £100 and something goes wrong, you should be able to get a refund from the credit-card provider.

However, if you do not pay in full, the interest cost can be high – up to 10% above bank base rate. There will be a limit to the amount you can have outstanding and you must pay 10% of the outstanding balance each month.*

If you are a regular user of your card for longer-term credit, make sure you have a competitive interest rate – compare the annual percentage rate (APR). Take account of when interest starts and whether there is still a free period if you have not paid in full.

Most cards can be used to draw cash, but in that case there is no interest-free period, so it is expensive.

Credit cards are particularly useful for paying when abroad. The charge is usually 1% on top of exchange rate difference – less than the cost of travellers' cheques or foreign

*If you are going to make a major purchase with your card, it is worth remembering the normal date of your monthly statement and if appropriate waiting a few days, to get another month's free credit.

currency purchase. However, you should try to avoid letting your card out of your sight when you pay, in case of fraud.

Summary points

★ Build up an emergency fund or arrange a borrowing facility.

★ If you have to borrow money, use the cheapest source and aim to pay it off quickly.

★ Consider reducing your mortgage.

★ Keep your bank accounts under control.

★ Use credit cards carefully and pay in full each month if possible.

3 Avoiding Financial Disaster

Insurance is expensive – a large portion of your premium goes to meet costs – but you need protection against financial losses you cannot afford.

In this chapter, six things that really matter:
~ Protecting your dependants if you die
~ Facing up to possible incapacity
~ Preparing for possible redundancy
~ Insuring your home ...
~ ... and contents
~ Car insurance

Risk management is taking action to prevent possible loss – fitting a burglar alarm is an example. Insurance is the last resort, because of the expense – up to a third of the premium goes to pay the insurer's costs, such as administration and claim handling.

In addition to avoiding financial disaster

there are two other areas where insurance may be necessary: for legal or contractual requirements. Car third-party insurance is required by law. A mortgage lender of over 75–80% of the property value may require mortgage protection insurance.*

Is this you?

• How can I make sure my family are provided for should I die? • I don't know what would happen if I had an accident preventing me from working. • I think I am going to be made redundant. • Does it matter if my house is under-insured? • I have indemnity cover on my house contents – what does it mean? • I damaged my car by backing into a wall – if I claim will I lose my no-claims bonus?

Protecting your dependants if you die

If you are a member of your employer's pension scheme it may well include a benefit if you die whilst still in service. If not, or if it

* *Insurance is cover against something that might happen, such as your house burning down. Assurance is cover against something that will happen, such as your death.*

is inadequate, consider some form of life assurance.*

Term

This is the cheapest form as it is for a limited period only. An example is a mortgage protection policy, which is for the life of the mortgage only. If it is a repayment mortgage it only need be on a reducing balance basis – as the mortgage is repaid – the cheapest form of all.

A more specialised example is a family income policy which, instead of a lump sum, pays a tax-free income to your dependants for the period covered.

Whole-life

This pays out when you die and so is more expensive. Premiums can stop at retirement. There will always be a cash-in value and the policy can be used as security against a loan.

Endowment

This usually arises in connection with mortgage repayment and it includes life

* *Statistics show that one in three people under the age of 30 will not live to 65, so family breadwinners should consider some way of protecting their dependants.*

cover. It is no longer thought to be a good way of saving to pay off a mortgage because of high charges and the risk that there will be a shortfall.

Facing up to possible incapacity

Incapacity to work can arise from sickness or accident. There is help from the state, but is it enough?

Sick pay

If you are employed, your employer pays you statutory sick pay, but it only continues for six months and the maximum at the time of going to press is only £62.20 a week.

Incapacity benefit

There is a state benefit for incapacity, tax free, but a medical check is required.

It is not payable if you are in receipt of statutory sick pay or if you are capable of doing any work, i.e. not only your former job.

Housing costs

The state gives help with mortgage interest payments and certain other housing costs if you are out of work, but you must be eligible for Income Support, which means a low income and savings of less than £8,000.

Sickness insurance

Your employer might give cover at a higher level than the maximum and/or for a longer period. If not, consider insurance. Your trade union might have a policy. Another source is a friendly society.

Insurance is available to cover sickness, incapacity and unemployment together and this might be more appropriate for you.

Credit insurance

This covers the risk of not being able to pay the interest on a loan (such as a mortgage, when it is called a mortgage protection policy) in the event of loss of income due to disability, illness or redundancy as well as death. It is expensive, but unless you have savings you should consider it.

It is not available to self-employed people and there can be difficulties in connection with redundancy. Check the wording and find out whether pre-existing health problems are covered.

Permanent health insurance

This covers permanent incapacity, which may be more important to you than life cover (you are 14 times more likely to be off work for more than six months than you are to die before 65). Employers sometimes provide cover for senior staff.

Critical illness insurance

This pays a lump sum if you contract one of a specified list of potentially terminal illnesses, such as cancer. But a combination of life cover and permanent health may be better, as the cover is wider.*

Give careful consideration to the help available from the state and decide whether you need (and can afford) additional cover.

Preparing for possible redundancy

Availability of state help

If you are made redundant you are entitled to

statutory redundancy pay from your employer if you have been employed for more than two years. There is no help for the self-employed.

This is based on age, length of service and your pay. The maximum eligible pay at the time of going to press is £220 per week and the maximum number of weeks 30, so the most anyone can get is £6,600.

Job-seekers' Allowance is paid for the first six months of unemployment, the current (2001) amount being £50.35 (£79 for a couple) if you are aged at least 25. It is not available to the self-employed. Thereafter Income Support takes over.*

Help with housing costs is also available to people out of work due to redundancy.

Taking out insurance

Sickness insurance and credit insurance (see above under incapacity) both extend to redundancy but there is currently no separate insurance available for the provision of income during unemployment.

* *It makes sound financial sense to make some preparations in case redundancy happens to you.*

Insuring your home ...

When taking out a policy, think about the level of excess (i.e. self-insurance) you are prepared to bear, compared with premium saved. Have you got security arrangements (an alarm system and outside lights) which can achieve a reduced premium?

Are you covered for subsidence? If not, is there any risk of it?

Read the general conditions carefully. Do you know for how long the house can remain unoccupied before cover ceases? Does the policy include property-owner's liability to third parties (e.g. if a tile falls on the postman's head) and does it extend to workmen such as decorators?*

* Avoid under-insurance, because it could affect any claim. Even if you started with a valuation and index-linking (adjustment for inflation) is built in, it is best to check the level of cover every few years. If you make any additions, such as a conservatory, remember to add the cost to the insured value.

... and contents

There are two types of contents insurance:

~ indemnity (the cheaper), which pays out current value only

~ new-for-old, which pays replacement costs.

If you can afford the latter, it is much better.

Have you ever been round your home, room by room, to assess the replacement cost of everything? If not, you are likely to find it is more than you thought. Don't forget things in your garage and garden shed.

Does the policy require special declarations for high-risk items like TV and video? Is there a requirement for special locks and security devices?

Optional extras

These include:

~ all-risks cover for things you take out of the home – cameras, clothing (does it cover theft from your car?)

~ money and credit cards

~ legal expenses

There is an advantage in having the same insurer for house and contents – it saves arguments over things like TV aerials – but not if it is cheaper to go elsewhere.

Car insurance

There are three levels of car insurance:

~ third party only – the basic legal
  requirement

~ third party, fire and theft (TPFT)

~ comprehensive, which adds accidental
  damage to TPFT.

The following factors affect the premium:

~ level of excess – usually there is a
  minimum

~ no-claims bonus, which can be protected
  by paying extra

~ car age, value and annual usage

~ whether the car is used for work

~ number of drivers and their ages

~ whether you have a garage

~ whether you have an alarm and/or
  immobiliser.

Check these points in the policy wording:

~ Does the insurer reserve the right to cancel the policy in the event of total loss?

~ Is a replacement provided if your car is under repair?

~ Do you lose your no-claims bonus even if an accident is not your fault?

~ Are windscreens excluded from no-claims bonus?

~ How much cover is there for personal items stolen from the car?

~ Are the insured drivers covered when driving another vehicle? (If so, it will be third party only.)

The possible loss of your no-claims bonus means you should consider carefully whether to make a claim for a relatively small loss, but any accident must be reported.*

Summary points

* Shop around for the best deal and read the small print.

★ Do you have cover for loss of income due to death or permanent incapacity of the breadwinner in your family?

★ Do you know how much statutory sick pay you are entitled to and for how long? Is it enough, or do you need insurance?

★ What about redundancy pay? Do you know your current entitlement? Do you need more cover?

★ It is dangerous to be under-insured. Have you checked your buildings cover recently? Have you included additions?

★ Have you been round your home to check the replacement value of the contents?

★ Are you aware of the provisions in your car insurance for no-claims bonus?

4 Financing Your Retirement

It is never too early nor too late to start paying into a pension scheme. Many pensions turn out to be less than expected.

In this chapter, six things that really matter:
- ~ Maximising the state pension
- ~ Joining an occupational pension scheme
- ~ Starting a personal pension
- ~ Making use of the new stakeholder pension
- ~ Understanding annuities
- ~ Planning for your retirement

With tax relief (2001), for those on a marginal tax rate of 22%, a pension contribution of £100 costs only £78 (and for those on 40% only £60). It then earns income free of income and capital gains tax (except that tax deducted from dividends cannot be recovered). So pensions are a very tax-efficient investment.

Income tax is, of course, deducted from

pensions in the course of payment, but a tax-free lump sum can often be taken on retirement.

A useful rough guide is that to achieve a pension of £20,000 a year starting from age 65, a man needs to pay about £250 a month if starting at age 30, £500 starting at 40 and £1,000 at 50. Women should add 10%.*

Is this you?

• My state basic pension will not be the full amount because I have missed contributions. Can I make them up? • I have been paying for a personal pension but my new employer has a company scheme. Should I join? • I am self-employed and haven't bothered about pensions until now. Should I start a personal pension? • I have no earned income and have been told I cannot pay into a pension scheme. Is that correct? • I am retiring shortly. Annuity rates are so low, should I delay taking one out? • How do I find out how much pension I will receive?

* *So it pays to start as early as possible, as funds are building up on a tax-free basis.*

Maximising the state pension

All state pensions are taxable and are adjusted annually in line with inflation.

Basic pension

A single contributor at the time of going to press receives £72.50 a week if full contributions have been made. A non-contributing spouse receives £43.40 a week.

A contributing spouse whose contributions have earned less can have their pension increased to £43.40. A widowed spouse can have their pension increased to the full amount received by the deceased spouse.

The pension can be left in after normal retiring age, up to age 70. It increases by 7.5% a year, which is not a very good deal as it takes some 12 years to recover the amount sacrificed.

Additional pension (SERPS)

This is paid in respect of each year you have made National Insurance contributions (NICs) in respect of earnings as an employee between the lower and upper earnings limits

– in 2001 £80 and £575 a week. It is not available to the self-employed.

The amount of pension payable is a complicated calculation. The formula changed with effect from April 2000 and will result in gradually lower amounts over the next few years. It is fully explained in a Benefits Agency booklet. There is a proposal to change to a flat-rate second state pension.

Contracting out

Many occupational schemes contract all members out of the additional pension. The scheme must guarantee a pension of no less than would have been received. Lower NICs are paid, the difference being called a rebate.

Employees who have a personal pension can also contract out if their scheme is an appropriate personal pension (APP). Instead of a rebate, the scheme receives a payment based on NICs, which must be claimed by the pension provider.*

* *Just before retirement age, you should receive a statement showing your state pension entitlement and thereafter a statement each year showing the annual increase.*

Joining an occupational pension scheme

These are schemes arranged by an employer for employees. There are two basic types: final salary and money purchase.

Final salary

The pension is based on the final pensionable salary (FPS), i.e. that received immediately before retirement, or a formula such as the average of the last three years.
It is the best form of pension for an employee, because the benefits are fixed. Usually the employee contribution is a fixed percentage of salary and the employer pays the rest.

The amount of pension is calculated by multiplying the FPS by a fraction in respect of each year of service, such as 1/60 which achieves a 50% pension after 30 years' service (called a 60ths scheme).

Money purchase

Here the contributions are fixed and the benefit varies, which is much less attractive to the employee but much more advantageous to the employer (many have switched new employees to money purchase). Most of the accumulated funds must eventually be used to buy an annuity.*

The disadvantage to the employee is twofold: not knowing in advance either how much the invested contributions will earn or what pension the final amount will purchase.

Questions to ask before joining

It is nearly always advantageous to join a company scheme, but first find out:

~ Is it final salary or money purchase?

~ Is it contracted out?

~ What are the contribution rates, for employer and employee?

~ Can a tax-free lump sum be taken on retirement?

~ Is there a contingent spouse's pension?

~ What happens in the event of death, in service or in retirement?

* An annuity is a guaranteed income for life. Part of the income is interest and part repayment of capital.

~ What happens if employment is ended by either party?

~ What would be the effect of being laid off without pay, or short-time working?

If it is a final-salary scheme:

~ How is the pension calculated?

~ Is there any post-retirement adjustment for inflation and is it guaranteed or discretionary?

~ What are the rules for early and late retirement and is there any difference if early retirement is due to ill-health?

Inland Revenue limits

Contributions to and income earned in an approved scheme are tax free if the following limits are not exceeded*

~ Maximum pensionable salary – for joiners since 14 March 1989, £95,400 (this is reviewed annually in the budget). No limit for earlier joiners.

* Company rules may impose lower amounts.

~ Maximum pension – two thirds of FPS (which can include fringe benefits).

~ Maximum for spouse on death of pensioner – two thirds of the maximum (i.e. 4/9ths of FPS).

~ Minimum service for maximum pension – 20 years (i.e. 30ths) for joiners since 17 March 1987, ten years if earlier.

~ Contribution limit for employee – 15% of salary (none for employer).

~ Post-retirement adjustment – full inflation.

~ Lump-sum cash – 2.25 times initial pension for joiners since 1 June 1988, 1.5 times FPS after 20 years' service (reduced in proportion if less service) for earlier joiners.

Hardly anyone reaches all these limits.

Early retirement

Pensions are lower if you retire early for two reasons – less service and earlier payment. The latter is dealt with by the application of an early-retirement factor (ERF) to the pension, usually at least 4% for each year not worked.

Many schemes waive the ERF in the case of ill-health early retirement and employers wishing to encourage early retirement may eliminate it by paying in extra.

Cash lump sum on retirement

Most schemes have an option to take a tax-free lump sum on retirement, the pension being reduced proportionally.*

If the pension is fully inflation proofed, then it might be better to leave the money in. Otherwise, check whether you can buy an annuity with the cash to provide a higher income.

Additional voluntary contributions (AVCs)

All schemes are required to have a facility for AVCs and anyone who can afford it and is not up to the Inland Revenue limits should consider making AVCs.

Additional benefits earned are usually on a money-purchase basis but may be in the form of additional years of service, which should be better.

* *'If you wish to pay off your mortgage, then it could be worth taking some of your pension out. But think carefully before you take it to buy a new car or a holiday.*

For AVCs commencing after 8 April 1987, it is not possible to take part as a lump sum. For this reason it is worth considering a stakeholder pension (see below) instead of some or all of your AVC, as it will then be possible to take the tax-free lump sum.

Free-standing AVCs (FSAVCs) are outside the company scheme. Whilst giving more freedom, they are probably more expensive as you must pay the administration costs instead of the company paying.

There is some debate about whether AVCs are better value than Individual Savings Accounts (ISAs). With AVCs the contributions are tax free, but the benefits are taxable. With ISAs it is the opposite. Most experts favour AVCs because the tax relief comes at the beginning, so funds accumulate on a tax-free basis. ISAs allow more freedom of action, but is this a good thing for pension money?*

* *If you are in a company pension scheme, consider making additional voluntary contributions, to increase your pension entitlement.*

Starting a personal pension

Personal pensions are suitable for people who cannot (or do not wish to) join a company scheme, the self-employed, those who change jobs frequently and those in irregular work. The basis is money purchase so there is no guarantee of benefit amount.

Contributions

These are usually paid regularly each month but can be irregular and some people prefer to wait until the year end to see how much they can afford.

A regular payment has a certain discipline but you are usually tied to a contract and charges tend to be higher. With lump sum payments will not be tied and so can seek the best deal each time. Either way, a flexible arrangement is sensible, so that you can increase or reduce contributions at will.

Contributions can be paid into an individual pension account (IPA) which is a 'wrapper' like an ISA and gives much greater control over how the money is invested.

Inland Revenue limits

Maximum contributions start at 17.5% of earnings and increase with age, up to 40%

for those over 60, subject to the same earnings limit as occupational schemes. There is no limit to the amount of the pension. The tax-free lump sum can be up to 25% of the fund.

Since April 2001, when stakeholder pensions came in, it is possible to make annual contributions of £3,600 to personal or stakeholder pensions, or both together, the earnings-related limits only applying to higher levels of contributions.

Personal pensions

Shop around with a list of questions:

~ How flexible can the contributions be?

~ What are the charges?

~ What are the penalties (if any) for stopping and transferring?

~ What happens if you die before buying an annuity – is your fund protected from inheritance tax?

~ Are there penalties if you buy your annuity elsewhere?

~ What is the past growth record of the fund you will be investing in?

~ How safe will your fund be?*

Retirement

After taking any tax-free cash, the balance of the fund must be used to buy an annuity. This can be done at any age between 50 and 75 and so can be postponed beyond retirement. The possible advantage of delay is that the stock market and/or annuity rates might improve.

If annuity purchase is deferred, income must be drawn directly from the fund within minimum and maximum percentages.

Deferment may be appropriate if you intend to work part time. Otherwise, experts suggest that it is not viable if your fund is below £100,000.

* Consider using an independent financial adviser (IFA) to help you choose a personal pension provider. Make sure they have the pension qualification. Ask about fees. Ring 0117 971 1177 for a list of IFAs in your area.

Making use of the new stakeholder pension

Stakeholder pensions were introduced in April

2001. Contribution limits are the same as for personal pensions. On retirement the fund must be used to buy an annuity but up to 25% can be taken as a tax-free lump sum.

In this case the Inland Revenue adds a tax rebate to your contributions equivalent to the standard rate of tax (i.e. in 2001 just over 28p for each £1) even if you pay no tax. Higher rate taxpayers can claim back the balance at the year end.

Annual charges will be capped at 1% of fund value, with no initial charges and no penalties for transferring the fund or suspending contributions.

Stakeholder pensions can be held alongside existing personal pensions or company schemes (but not where the employee earns more than £30,000 a year in the case of final-salary schemes). Contributions can be paid into an individual pension account (IPA) which is a 'wrapper' like an ISA and gives much greater control over how the money is invested.*

* *If you have a personal pension, it might be worthwhile switching your first £3,600 of annual contributions to a stakeholder pension, because of the tight rules on charges.*

Understanding annuities

As already explained, money purchase, personal and stakeholder pension funds must eventually be used to buy an annuity. This is called a compulsory purchase annuity (CPA) and all the receipts are taxable.

Voluntary purchase of an annuity – such as with the tax-free lump sum – is called a purchased life annuity (PLA) and only the interest element of the receipts are taxable (the capital refund element is about half the receipts).

There is a wide choice of type of annuity, such as single life, joint life, impaired life (where you have a potentially terminal health problem, leading to higher rates) and they can be flat-rate or indexed. It is also possible to have an annuity based on the stock market, with variable returns.

* *The best annuity rates can be found in weekend newspapers, or telephone the Annuity Bureau on 020 7620 4090.*

There is also a wide variety of rates for each type, so make sure your pension provider gives you all the alternatives and makes it clear whether there is any penalty for shopping around. Because women on average live longer than men, their rates are lower.*

Planning for your retirement

Get a forecast of your state pension entitlement about five years before you intend to retire, to see if you can get more by making additional contributions – ask your local DSS office for an application form.

Shortly before retirement occupational schemes normally provide a quote showing your pension and that is when you decide about taking a cash lump sum.*

With a personal pension the provider will tell you the lump sum available and give an indication of annuity rates. This is when you decide whether to defer taking the pension.

Prepare a new income and expenditure budget for after retirement. Consider whether to use your lump sum to reduce your mortgage.

A year or two before retirement, review your investments to see if you should start switching from growth to income investments.

* *Many employers offer pre-retirement courses, books or magazines. Take advantage of any such offers.*

Summary points

★ Do you know your state pension position, especially if you are nearing retirement?

★ Have you considered making AVCs to supplement your company pension?

★ Consider switching your personal pension if the charges are high.

★ Can you take advantage of the new stakeholder pension?

★ If you have to buy an annuity with your pension money, give careful consideration as to which type of annuity is best for you.

★ If nearing retirement, have you prepared a post-retirement income and expenditure budget, to see where you stand?

5 Controlling Tax and Benefits

You need to understand the basic tax and benefits rules to ensure you receive all the allowances, reliefs and benefits you are entitled to.

In this chapter, five things that really matter:
- ~ Attacking your income tax bill
- ~ Reducing National Insurance contributions
- ~ Benefiting from social security
- ~ Minimising capital gains tax
- ~ Avoiding inheritance tax

For employees, income tax (IT) is deducted from pay by the pay-as-you-earn (PAYE) system, which spreads the impact evenly over the year. The self-employed do not have this convenience.

Some people look upon National Insurance contributions (NICs) as contributions to a fund rather like pensions. This is wrong. There is no fund and there are no rights to future benefits. Consequently you should recognise

NICs as in effect another tax on income.

Capital gains tax (CGT) is payable on the sale not only of stocks and shares but also of anything other than household goods and personal effects up to the value of £6,000 and private motor vehicles. Subject to certain exceptions, you do not pay CGT on any gain you make when you sell your home. Nor, on the other hand, can you set off any loss against gains made elsewhere.

Inheritance tax (IHT) is normally payable on death but can be partly payable earlier. It is also sometimes called a voluntary tax, because there are so many ways of avoiding it, but they are not straightforward.*

Is this you?

• I am getting married next month – will we get the married couple's allowance? • How do I get these new tax credits? • I am becoming self employed – how will my National Insurance contributions be paid? • How do I work out the taxable gain when I sell some shares? • If my husband and I leave

* Do not expect the tax and benefit authorities to know all about your situation. How can they unless you tell them?

everything to each other, will we avoid inheritance tax?

Attacking your income tax bill

Allowances

Apart from the personal allowance (in 2001 £4,535), there is a married couple's allowance for certain pensioners and a blind person's allowance.

Reliefs

Reliefs from income tax arise in respect of certain payments that you make and are deducted from income in arriving at taxable income. They include:

~ Interest on loans – mortgage interest relief has been abolished but you can claim tax relief on certain other loans, such as to buy or improve the property you rent.

~ Pension scheme contributions.

~ Expenses at work – if you are employed and you have to pay for:

  – things you use at work, such as tools

or working clothes
- travelling expenses or use of your car on company business (but not from home to work)
- subscriptions to professional bodies.

~ Renting a room – if you rent out furnished accommodation in your only or main home and receive less than (2001) £4,250 a year gross income, i.e. before deducting expenses, it is tax free.

~ Maintenance payments – pensioners entitled to the married couple's allowance get relief on maintenance payments, subject to the same limits.

~ Charitable payments – every payment to a charity now qualifies for recovery by the charity of the tax deducted. If you are a higher rate taxpayer, you receive a tax rebate for the balance.

Taxable income

After deducting your allowances and reliefs, what is left is taxable income. This is subject to tax at increasing rates for successive bands, at the time of going to press:

Lower rate band	10%	Up to £1,880
Basic rate band	22%	£1,881 to £29,400
Higher rate band	40%	Over £29,400*

Tax credits

These have replaced certain National Insurance benefits. They are paid through the PAYE system. They have to be applied for on forms available from Benefits Agency offices, job centres, post offices and tax enquiry centres, as well as Citizens' Advice Bureaux. Tax credits include:

~ Working families' tax credit – available to couples (or single parents) with one or more children living with them. One parent must be working for at least 16 hours a week and savings cannot be more than £8,000.

~ Disabled person's tax credit – the disabled person must be working for at least 16 hours a week and savings cannot be more than £16,000.

~ Children's tax credit – despite the name,

The bands tend to be increased each year in line with inflation. The rates are changed from time to time.

this is an allowance rather than a credit. Families with at least one child will get 10% relief on £5,200, subject to a reduction if the claimant pays higher-rate tax.

Investment income

Income from the following investments is free of tax:

~ National Savings Certificates and children's bonus bonds

~ TESSAs (till maturity)

~ PEPs

~ ISAs

~ Friendly Society savings schemes.

Dividends on shares are treated as having been taxed at source at 10% (this is sometimes called the dividend tax credit). It cannot be avoided and cannot be recovered by a non-taxpayer. Higher-rate taxpayers must pay a further 32.5%.

Tax-free benefits in kind

Find out if any are provided by your employer. Can you persuade your employer to provide some, bearing in mind that they are also free of National Insurance contributions for the employer.

The following are tax free:

~ Company contributions to occupational or (within limits) personal pensions.

~ Loans – an employer can make a loan to an employee of up to £5,000 at no interest or at a low rate of interest. Above that amount, a set rate of interest (in 2001 7.75%) is used to calculate the taxable benefit.

~ Relocation costs – if your employer moves you to another area, you can receive reimbursement of relocation costs totalling up to £8,000 tax free. Beyond that it becomes a taxable benefit.

~ Golden handshakes – statutory redundancy pay is tax free and if you receive additional compensation, up to £30,000 may be tax free. There are complicated rules.

~ Mobile phones.

Spouses

There are various ways that a married couple can minimise their joint tax liabilities, by making full use of both personal allowances and lower tax rates.

If one is self-employed, could the other receive pay from the business, perhaps by performing clerical tasks? Could the business be in joint ownership so that the profits are shared?

Where one spouse is employed and the other is not, the only way of transferring income is by putting savings in the name of the one who is unemployed, so that they receive the income.

Money can be freely transferred. Shares or units can be transferred between spouses (but not between unmarried couples) without payment, although the transfer must be unconditional. All that is required is the preparation of a standard share transfer form (obtainable from any law stationer). It must be stamped, but only at 50p.*

* Apart from the free transfer of shares, all these steps can be taken by an unmarried couple.

The married couple's allowance (now only available to pensioners) is normally received by the husband, but can be transferred to the wife. However, since the allowance is limited to 10%, this action would save tax only if the wife does but the husband does not pay income tax.

Children

Children are liable for income tax and are entitled to the personal allowance and the lower rates. Parents can only transfer to a child capital which earns no more than £100 a year. If income from transferred capital exceeds that amount, it is treated as income of the parent and is taxed accordingly.

Since the limit only applies to parents, there is nothing to prevent grandparents (or anyone else) from transferring capital to a child, although the inheritance tax rules apply.

Loss-making business

If you have an expensive hobby you might be able to turn it into a loss-making business.

Then losses can be set against other taxable income, thus reducing tax liability.

Professional advice is advisable. You need to be trading so that there is some way, or potential way, of earning income.

Annual planning

It is worth reviewing your situation before the end of each tax year (i.e. before 5 April).

Check whether there have been any changes in your personal position which can affect your tax liability. Are there any allowances or reliefs you can claim which you have previously overlooked?*

Reducing National Insurance contributions

National Insurance contributions (NICs) are paid on earnings, not unearned income. Consequently any replacement of earnings by unearned income reduces your NICs.

In the case of benefits-in-kind for employees, tax-free benefits are generally free of NICs. Taxable benefits are not.

* It is possible to go back up to six years in order to recover overpaid tax. Leaflets on all tax subjects are available from your Tax Office.

The main limitation on fringe benefits is that they must be convertible neither into cash nor reimbursements. For example, a season ticket paid for by the employer is free of NICs, but if the ticket is bought by the employee who is then reimbursed, then NICs are payable.

Petrol for private use must by paid for by company voucher or company credit card. Alcoholic liquor is specifically made subject to NICs.

Examples of fringe benefits free of NICs are:

~ board and lodging

~ clothing

~ gifts of tangible items (not money) in respect of long-service awards, birthday or retirement presents

~ luncheon vouchers

~ club membership fees

~ fees to professional bodies (if membership is a condition of employment)

So there is clearly an advantage in receiving fringe benefits instead of pay.

~ medical insurance

~ school fees.*

Benefiting from social security

The main benefits are:

~ Child benefit – payable for each child under 16 or, if in full-time education, 19. There are no limits or deductions; every child is eligible.

~ Income support – payable if you work for less than 16 hours a week. There are income and savings limits.

~ Council tax benefit – for those who receive income support.

~ Housing benefit – for those who pay rent and receive income support.

Other benefits include incapacity benefit, attendance allowance, industrial death or injury, maternity and widows benefit.

In addition, those in receipt of other benefits may qualify for help with NHS costs, such as prescriptions, dental and optical costs.*

* *Leaflets on all these can be obtained from your local Benefits Office.*

Minimising capital gains tax

Capital losses are set off against capital gains in the same tax year and after that there is an annual exemption, currently £7,500. As a result, few people pay capital gains tax (CGT).

If the net result of a year's transactions (before the annual exemption) is a loss, it can be carried forward to succeeding years. The annual exemption cannot be carried forward, but can be applied to the net gains for a year before any loss brought forward which, if not then used, can be carried forward again.

The following investments are exempt:

~ gilt-edged stock

~ company debentures and loan stocks

~ ISAs and PEPs

~ permanent interest-bearing shares of building societies (PIBs)

~ enterprise investment schemes and venture capital trusts (EIS and VCTs).

Indexation and taper relief

For purchases before April 1998 the cost can be indexed, that is adjusted by the cumulative rate of inflation (RPI) between purchase and April 1998. However, indexation cannot be taken beyond break-even, i.e. it cannot be used to create a loss.*

From April 1998, indexation was replaced by taper relief which is based on length of ownership. It only applies to shares held for at least three complete years, although an extra year is added to the total for shares owned on 17 March 1998.

The percentage of the gain chargeable reduces to 95% after the third complete year and by a further 5% for each successive year, to a minimum of 60% after ten complete years.

For example, if you bought shares in August 1996 and sold them in June 2001, the taxable gain would be calculated as follows:

~ the original cost would be increased to 5 April 1998 in accordance with the CGT indexation allowance for the period, to give the indexed cost

* *The Inland Revenue leaflet on CGT includes a table of CGT indexation allowances for April 1998.*

~ the excess of the selling value over the indexed cost gives the taxable gain before taper relief

~ although the shares have only been held for two full years since April 1998, as the shares were held on 17 March 1998 an extra year is added, making a total of three years, so taper relief reduces the chargeable gain to 95%.

More favourable taper relief applies to business assets and since 6 April 2000 it also applies to all shares owned in your employing company and to all shares in unquoted and AIM quoted companies.

The percentage of the gain chargeable in this case reduces to 87.5% after the first complete year, to 75% after two years and 50% after three, to a minimum of 25% after four years.

Where shares qualify as business assets only from 6 April 2000, the gain for shares owned on that date has to be apportioned between the two periods.

The complications of indexation and taper relief can of course be ignored if your total gains for a year do not exceed the annual exemption, currently £7,500.

Re-investment relief

Chargeable gains on disposals can be deferred indefinitely if the amounts realised are re-invested in new share issues from qualifying companies under the Enterprise Investment Scheme.*

Annual planning

This is mainly a matter of ensuring you make use of your annual tax-free allowance.

You should keep a running record of your sales during each financial year (starting 6 April), with a note of the gain or loss, after adjusting for indexation and taper relief.

Check on the cumulative position at the beginning of March. If you have a substantial amount of your annual allowance still available, then take a look at the unrealised gains in your portfolio.

* See chapter 6 under other tax-efficient investments.

Bed and breakfasting

Before 17 March 1998, any unused annual

allowance could be applied to unrealised gains before the end of the tax year by selling the shares one day and buying them back the next. This has been stopped by introducing a 30-day interval between selling and buying back, otherwise the two transactions will be ignored for capital gains tax purposes.

It is, of course, possible to take the risk of being out of the market for 30 days. Other alternatives are:

~ If you have not used all your current year's ISA allowance or have uninvested amounts in a PEP, then you can 'bed and ISA' or 'bed and PEP', that is buy back into an ISA or PEP.

~ If you are married you can sell and your spouse buy back (or vice versa).

~ You can buy a similar share (e.g. BP for Shell) or your best choice of new investment.

With all these alternatives the sale and buy-back can be done simultaneously, so there is no risk of adverse price movement overnight.

The disadvantage is that costs of both selling and buying (including stamp duty) are incurred, although some stockbrokers will forgo some or all of their commission on the second transaction. Also, you lose the difference between the buying and selling prices.*

Avoiding inheritance tax

Making gifts during your lifetime

Inheritance tax (IHT) may be payable on gifts you make before your death but, if you can afford it, there are a number of gifts you can make free of IHT. Of particular importance is the £3,000 annual exemption (higher amounts on marriage) and the unlimited number of gifts of £250 to any one person.

Gifts to individuals or certain trusts that are not otherwise exempt are potentially exempt transfers (PETs). Tax is avoided if you live for seven years after making the gift, but if not it may be payable on your death.

Gifts to companies or discretionary trusts are called immediately chargeable transfers

* *If you have investments, do you keep adequate records to enable you to calculate the capital gain when you sell? If not, make an effort to put it right now.*

(ICTs) and half the IHT rate of 40% is payable immediately. The balance may become payable if you die within seven years but if no tax is due then you cannot recover what has been paid.

Tax payable on death

Amounts left to your spouse are free of IHT and most couples leave everything to each other, but this may not be the best solution.

The first £242,000 of taxable estate (the exempt amount or threshold) is free of tax. It sounds a lot but with house values now so high, tax may be payable. Beyond the threshold, the tax rate is 40%.

PETs and ICTs made within seven years of your death are counted in order of payment and so are set against the threshold first. There is taper relief from the fourth year but it only applies to amounts which exceed the threshold.

Tax must be paid before grant of probate (official permission for executors to act) but assets cannot be sold before getting probate, so it may be necessary for the executor(s) to borrow.

If the estate includes property, it is possible to defer payment of the proportion of IHT payable that is equal to the proportion of the property value to the whole estate.

Certain investments that include life cover, such as with-profits bonds, although subject to IHT, can be written into trust so that they pass directly to your heirs and can then be realised to meet at least some of the tax bill.

Planning for IHT

The importance of making a will cannot be over-stressed. Otherwise, intestacy rules apply, which may not suit you.*

* Make a will and also leave an explanation of it and instructions regarding other matters, ranging from whether you wish to be buried or cremated to where you keep your building society passbook.

If a married couple's joint estate may exceed the threshold, they need to find a way of using the exempt amount on the first death. The problem usually is that the survivor cannot manage without the assets, particularly the house.

There are ways in which this problem can be overcome but they need to be watertight, so the use of a solicitor experienced in IHT planning is essential. Usually a trust is set up to come into operation on the first death and receive assets up to the exempt amount. It is possible for the surviving spouse to be a beneficiary.

If all the beneficiaries agree, a will can be changed within two years of the death – this is called a deed of variation.

If you know that IHT will be payable, make some provision for it, such as life assurance. For a married couple, a joint life second death policy can be taken out, written into trust for the beneficiaries so that it escapes the IHT net.

Summary points

★ Check your income tax position shortly before the year end to make sure you have all the allowances and reliefs you are entitled to.

★ Are your fringe benefits subject to National Insurance contributions because they are convertible into cash? If so, can you do anything about it?

★ Are you aware of the social security benefits you may qualify for? If not, get hold of leaflets from your local office.

★ Capital gains tax liability should also be looked at before the year end to see whether you can sensibly use your exempt amount.

★ If you have a potential inheritance tax liability, think about taking steps to reduce it, or at least provide for it.

6 Investing Savings

The most important point when investing savings is to spread the risk over a number of different investments so that your fortunes are not dependent on one product.

In this chapter, six things that really matter:
~ Understanding investing
~ Selecting the investment period
~ Choosing tax-efficient investments
~ Other suitable investments for savings
~ Lump-sum investing
~ Investing as a non-taxpayer

There are many investment products that accept regular monthly payments.

In other cases, where the minimum investment is low, and monthly savings are high enough, they can be invested directly. For example, National Savings certificates have a minimum of £100.

Otherwise, savings can be put into deposit

accounts until enough has been accumulated to make a lump-sum investment.

'Real' rates of interest, the difference between actual interest earned and the rate of inflation, are important. Since all interest is taxable, high interest rates can result in negative real rates.*

Is this you?

• I have savings to invest but am nervous about seeking advice because I know I will not understand. • I can save money but I just leave it in a building society. • First there were TESSAs and PEPs; now there are ISAs – what are they? • Are National Savings good investments? • What is the difference between a unit trust and an investment trust? • I don't pay tax; what investments are suitable for me?

Understanding investing

Fixed interest investments

These are investments where the income is a

* *The advantage of investing regular savings is that there need be no commitment to maintaining payments – e.g. there is no harm done by missing a monthly purchase of a savings certificate.*

fixed amount, at least for the time being. Usually the capital value is also fixed, although in some cases it can change, too. However, either income or capital are fixed.

Equities

These are investments in ordinary shares of companies, where both the income and the capital can vary up or down.

They can be bought and sold on a stock exchange and they participate in profits and receive dividends, which are usually paid half-yearly.

Fixed interest versus equities

All statistics show that in the long run, due to capital growth, equities beat fixed interest investments by a big margin, whereas fixed interest may not even beat inflation.

Although the income on equities is less than on fixed interest to start with, it catches up and passes it in the long run.

But to achieve the best returns on equities, it is necessary to have flexibility in the timing of both buying and selling.

Risk

The more you have invested and the longer you can leave it alone, the more risk you can afford to take with some of it, to achieve a higher reward. The most important thing is to recognise the existence of risk and to take appropriate steps.

Spread your investments over a number of different categories, having perhaps more than one investment in each category. Consider pooled investments such as unit trusts.

Choosing an investment category

The issues to consider are :

~ Do you want protection against inflation? Equities stand a better chance of achieving it in the long run and index-linked products can be considered for fixed-interest investing.

~ Do you want income? Income-producing equity investments can achieve growth as well.

~ Can you afford to take risks?

Questions to ask about any investment

~ Capital – does it remain unchanged or can it go up and down?

~ Income – is it fixed or variable? Is it paid out, kept in or reinvested ?

~ Tax – is income tax-free, taxable or taxed? Are capital gains taxable ?

~ Guarantees of income or capital – are there any?

~ Period of investment – is it fixed or variable?

~ Risks to capital or income – what are they?

~ Commission – is any payable and to whom?

~ Management fees – how much, if any. Are they initial and/or annual?

~ Past performance – what is it, remembering that it may not be maintained?

~ Future performance – what could affect it?

Monitoring your investments

It is essential to keep records: date of purchase or sale, quantity, price and value.

It is also a good idea to record successive prices, where appropriate, so you can spot a trend.

Another vital record is a diary of future events, such as the date National Savings certificates expire.*

Selecting the investment period

If your saving objective is short-term, such as for a holiday or Christmas, a bank or building society deposit account is best. Instant access may not be necessary, so you could use a notice account, if you can get higher interest. From two or three months up to a year might be appropriate.

If you are saving for a period beyond, say, one year ahead, such as for a family wedding, fixed interest is probably still best. There are deposit accounts available for periods beyond one year. Alternatives are National Savings products such as savings certificates.

* *If you have a computer, there are a number of programs for keeping records, and share prices can be downloaded and graphs drawn as an aid to investment decisions.*

Because equity investments achieve much higher returns than fixed interest in the long run, they are very suitable for investment periods of at least five years, such as for your children's education or for your retirement.*

Choosing tax-efficient investments

If you are a taxpayer you should first consider investments that are tax-efficient.

Short/medium term

National Savings with tax-free interest

Savings certificates are of two kinds: fixed interest and index-linked. They have two terms: two years and five years. The minimum is £100.

Children's bonus bonds can be bought in units of £25 for a child (under 16).

Premium bonds can be bought £100 at a time.

* As the objective gets closer, you should consider locking in your gains by gradually transferring your savings into fixed interest.

Longer term

Individual savings accounts (ISAs)

Most ISAs have savings schemes. The annual limit for investment is £7,000. Income and capital gains are tax free and dividends receive a 10% tax credit until 2004.

Investments can be of up to £3,000 in a cash component, £1,000 in an insurance component and up to the full £7,000 in stocks and shares.

Friendly societies

Friendly societies offer a tax-free investment linked to life assurance. The maximum investment is £25 a month or £270 a year. Income and capital gains in the scheme are free of tax and after ten years no tax is payable on withdrawal.

They are often promoted for children as they are a way of involving children's savings in equities, but most children are in a tax-free position anyway.

Savings-related share option schemes

If your employer has a scheme you should

consider joining. as the tax-free benefits are significant. Options are given to buy shares at the current market price (sometimes even at a discount) at a later date, when hopefully the value has risen. Meanwhile, savings are made to pay for the options through a save-as-you-earn (SAYE) scheme with a bank or building society.*

Other suitable investments for savings

Taxable National Savings

Most have minimum investment levels too high for direct investment of savings. The exception is capital bonds, which have a minimum of £100. They have only one term – five years – and the interest is kept in.

Unit trusts

These are a form of pooled investment consisting of a portfolio of shares managed by a professional company but owned separately by a trust. The price of a unit is the total value of the underlying investments divided by the number of units.

* *Make the most of the opportunities for tax-free investing, particularly if you are a higher-rate taxpayer, but do not make such an investment just because it is tax free – it must be worthwhile in itself.*

There may be an initial charge (up to 5%) included in the buying price. In some cases there is an exit charge instead, which reduces over a period. There is also an annual charge, usually 1%.

Most unit trust providers have regular savings plans for their products.*

Lump-sum investing

When a lump sum has been accumulated in a deposit account it can be used to buy any investment. The following have not so far been mentioned:

National Savings

Products with a minimum of £500 include:

~ Fixed Rate Savings Bonds, which have lives of six months, 12 months, and two years. Interest can be taken out or left in and is taxed.

Remember that in the long run, equity investments do better than fixed interest.

~ Pensioners' bonds for people over 60, with interest rates guaranteed for one, two or five years. Interest is paid monthly and is taxable.

~ Income bonds, with variable taxable
interest paid out monthly.

Gilts

These are British government fixed-interest
stocks. The most important factors are the
interest rate and the redemption (repayment)
date. There are a few stocks that have no
redemption date.

The interest rate is fixed for each stock (or
in some cases is index-linked) and, as they are
traded on the Stock Exchange, the price goes
up and down in accordance with prevailing
interest rates. These movements become less
as redemption date approaches.

The yield (interest as a percentage of
current market price) is expressed in two
ways – interest only and redemption, the
latter also taking into account the time till
redemption and the difference between the
current price and the redemption price.

Interest is paid out half-yearly and is
taxable (capital gains are not taxable).

Company fixed interest

These operate like gilts as the interest rate is fixed and so the stock market price varies. Interest is taxable but capital gains are tax free.

Guaranteed income bonds

These are managed investments which guarantee a relatively high return over a period, such as five years. The problem with them is that the capital value can be eroded.

With-profits bonds

These are pooled investments in the with-profits funds of life assurance companies, which are invested in a mixture of fixed interest, equities and property.

There is usually a minimum investment period (often five years), with penalties for earlier termination. Annual bonuses are declared but some growth is retained to smooth out returns and pay for terminal bonuses.

Direct investing in equities

It is advisable to spread your money over, say, ten companies, which means having at least £10,000 to invest, as it is not economic to put less than about £1,000 in any one, due to minimum dealing costs.

To spread the risk wider, shares can be bought in investment trusts, which are companies whose business is buying, holding and selling shares in other companies, so they make the investment decisions for you.*

Investing as a non-taxpayer

If you do not pay income tax, avoid investments where the interest or dividend is paid after tax is deducted and the tax cannot be recovered.

Tax-free investments are not necessarily advantageous to the non-taxpayer; taxable investments on which the tax can be avoided or recovered might offer a better return.

Tax is deducted from bank and building society interest at 20% before it is paid but non-taxpayers can arrange to receive it gross

* If you are starting equity investing, first consider pooled investments such as unit trusts rather than individual shares.

by completing a form obtainable from the provider stating that their total income is below the personal allowance.*

Summary points

★ Remember that the return on equities easily beats fixed interest over the long run.

★ Relate the term of your investment to your objectives.

★ Avoiding tax on income and/or capital gains is an attractive proposition but the saving needs to exceed any additional cost.

★ Regular savings are particularly suitable for equity investment because of pound/cost averaging – when the stock market is low, you get more shares or units than when it is high, so that the average price for each is lower than the average of the prices each time you invest.

★ Do not put all your investment eggs in

* *The non-taxpayer needs to look at returns on a pre-tax basis.*

one basket – aim for a balanced portfolio including both fixed interest and equities.

★ It is better for non-taxpayers to get interest paid gross than having to wait till the year end before tax deducted can be recovered.